Written by Neil Morris

Cartoons by Mark Davis

Miles Kelly
PUBLISHING

Projects created by
Ting Morris

Art director
Clare Sleven

Design
Mackerel Design

Project management
Mark Darling

Artwork commissioned by
Lynne French, Susanne Grant, Natasha Smith

Art reference
Lesley Cartlidge, Liberty Mella

Editorial director
Paula Borton

First published in 2000 by
Miles Kelly Publishing Ltd
Bardfield Centre, Great Bardfield, Essex CM7 4SL
Reprinted 2001

2468109753

British Library Cataloguing-in-Publication Data
A catalogue record for this book is available from the British Library

ISBN 1-90294-737-1

Printed in Hong Kong

Acknowledgements

The publishers wish to thank the following artists who have contributed to
this book:
Lisa Alderson (Advocate), Andy Becket (Illustration Ltd.), Martin Camm,
Mick Loates (Linden Artists), Terry Riley, Rudi Vizi.

All photographs from Miles Kelly Archives.

e-mail: info@mileskelly.net
www.mileskelly.net

CONTENTS

MAMMALS

Mammals form a large group of animals. They live all over the world, in hot countries as well as in freezing polar lands. Most mammals live on land, but whales and dolphins are mammals and they live in the sea.

Baby mammals are fed with milk from their mother's body, and an adult mammal has hair or fur to keep it warm.

☞ *Rock hyraxes live in colonies in Africa and the Middle East.*

Deer and fawn

Mother pig suckling piglets

Factfile

- Farmyard pigs are descended from wild boars.
- There are more than 4,000 different species (or kinds) of mammals.
- The hippopotamus secretes an oily pink fluid which protects it from sunburn.
- Mammals are warm-blooded animals.
- Bats are the only mammals that can fly.
- The pronghorn antelope can sustain a speed of 56 km/h for up to six km.

Hippo

Quiz

1 Are cats and dogs *mammals*?
2 Which is the largest *mammal*?
3 Which is the slowest *mammal*?
4 What is a baby horse called?
5 What are prickly porcupines covered with?
6 Which animal does bacon come from?

Answers
1 Yes. 2 Blue whale. 3 Sloth. 4 Foal. 5 Spines or quills. 6 Pig.

HUMANS ARE MAMMALS TOO!

Mammal mix-up

1. Everyone draws the head of their favourite mammal on a piece of paper. Draw it with a long neck.

2. Everyone folds over the paper, so that only the neck shows, and passes it on to the next player. Without looking under the fold, each player adds a body to the neck.

3. Everyone now folds and passes on. Each player now draws legs and feet/paws and passes on.

4. Now unfold the paper. What's happened to everyone's mammal? What a mix-up!

APES & MONKEYS

There are four different kinds of apes. Gorillas and chimpanzees live only on the continent of Africa. Orang-utans and gibbons live in Southeast Asia. Though they are similar to monkeys, apes are larger and have no tails.

There are lots of different monkeys. Many monkeys live in the rainforests of Africa and Asia, alongside apes. The new-world monkeys of Central and South America have long tails, which they use like an extra arm to swing through the trees.

Chimpanzees

MORE TEA DR. LIVINGSTONE?

Orang-utan

Quiz

1   Which group of animals is closest to man in development?

2   Are baboons apes or monkeys?

3   Which is the smallest ape?

4   What are the world's noisiest monkeys called?

5   Which ape's name means "man of the forest"?

6   Where do snow monkeys live?

Answers
1 Apes. 2 Monkeys. 3 Gibbon.
4 Howler monkeys.
5 Orang-utan. 6 Japan.

Monkey mobile

1. Make a collection of monkey pictures.

2. Look through old magazines, catalogues, birthday cards, or draw your own monkeys.

3. Cut them out and stick them on card.

4. Hang the pictures from a wire coat-hanger using cotton thread.

COATHANGER

COTTON THREAD

Gibbon

Gorilla

Factfile

- As the world's rainforests are being destroyed, many apes and monkeys are finding it difficult to survive.

- Gorillas are the largest apes; some are the same height as a tall man.

- Chimps use sticks as tools, to dig insects out of their nests.

- A kind of marmoset monkey that had never been seen by people before was found in Brazil in 1996.

- Gibbons can leap distances of up to 15 m between trees.

ELEPHANTS

There are just two different kinds of elephants – African and Asian (which are also called Indian elephants). African elephants are the world's biggest land animals. Males can grow over twice as tall as a man. Asian elephants are smaller and lighter.

Elephants live in family groups, and families often join together to make up large herds. Each herd is led by a female elephant, who is usually the oldest. She decides which route the herd should follow every day.

Factfile

- An elephant's tusks are really two big teeth made of ivory.

- Asian elephants are used in the logging industry, because they can carry very heavy loads.

- Elephants love to wallow in cool mud, which helps to protect their skin.

- Elephants do not have very good eyesight, but their hearing and sense of smell are excellent.

- An African elephant can weigh up to seven tonnes – as much as 90 people.

 The African elephant has larger ears than the Asian.

Quiz

1 Can elephants swim?

2 What is the word for a large group of elephants living together?

3 What is an elephant's long, bendy nose called?

4 Which aeroplane is named after an elephant?

5 Do elephants eat meat?

6 What are baby elephants called?

Answers

1 Yes. 2 Herd. 3 Trunk. 4 Jumbo jet 5 No. 6 Calves.

Elephant chain

1. Fold a long sheet of paper backwards and forwards into wide zigzags.

2. Copy an elephant onto the top page of the zigzag, with the tail joined to one edge and the trunk joined to the other.

FOLDED PAPER

3. Now cut around the outline carefully.

4. Draw ears and eyes, and colour them in.

5. Open out your elephant chain. All the elephants are holding trunks and tails.

The Indian elephant is an endangered species. There are now less than 40,000 left in the wild.

CATS

Our pet cats at home are relatives of the big cats that live in the wild. All cats are carnivores, which means that they eat meat. They have powerful bodies to help them move fast to hunt their prey. They have excellent eyesight and a good sense of smell.

Most big cats live alone or in pairs, but lions live together in groups, called prides. Male lions like to sit around and let the lionesses do most of the hunting.

👆 In a pride of lions, lionesses spend a lot of time looking after their cubs.

👈 Leopards are the most widespread of the big cats. They can be found in Africa, the Middle East and Asia.

Quiz

1 What are baby tigers called?
2 What does a male lion have around his neck?
3 What noise does a pet cat make?
4 Which big cat lives in the rainforests of Central and South America?
5 Do lions and lionesses look the same?
6 Which is bigger, a tiger or a tigress?

Answers
1 Cubs. 2 Mane. 3 Miaow.
4 Jaguar. 5 No. 6 Tiger.

Paper plate cat masks

PAPER PLATE

ELASTIC

1. Turn yourself into a big cat with a paper plate and paints. Cut a nose hole and slits for eyes. Paint a cat face – a tiger or a lion.

2. Stick on paper ears and wool whiskers. Yellow and orange crêpe paper strips make a good lion's mane.

3. Make a hole at each side of the plate and loop elastic bands through the holes. Slip the bands over your ears and roar away!

WOOL WHISKERS

The cheetah is the fastest land mammal over short distances, reaching its top speed of 100 km/h from a standing start in just three seconds.

Factfile

- Tigers are the biggest cats, reaching up to 3.7 m from head to tail.

- Pumas are also called cougars or mountain lions.

- A leopard's spots and a tiger's stripes let them blend in with their surroundings; this is called camouflage.

- A tiger eats about six tonnes of meat a year, which is the same as about 60,000 burgers!

- Most cats avoid water, but tigers like to swim.

BEARS

Bears are big, strong mammals. There are eight different kinds, and most are omnivorous, which means that they eat meat and plants. Brown bears live in forests in North America, Europe and Asia. In America they are usually called grizzlies, and they often live near American black bears. Asian black bears, sun bears, sloth bears and spectacled bears live in different parts of the world. Polar bears live only in the frozen Arctic.

The Polar bear is the only bear which actively preys on humans.

Grizzly bears can run at 50 km/h and weigh up to half a tonne.

Factfile

- The bear's closest relatives are racoons and dogs.

- Polar bears are very strong swimmers and can stay underwater for up to two minutes.

- There are a few wild brown bears still left in the Pyrenees mountains, between France and Spain.

- Spectacled bears, so called after their eye markings, live in the forests of the Andes mountains in South America.

- Many black bears are black, but some have brown, grey or bluish fur.

Quiz

1 Which is the largest kind of bear?

2 Can brown bears stand up on two legs?

3 Which bear is also called a dog bear or a honey bear?

4 What is a polar bear's favourite prey?

5 Where do the largest brown bears live?

6 What food do pandas eat?

Answers

1 Polar bear.
2 Yes. 3 Sun bear
4 Ringed seals.
3 Kodiak Island. 6 Bamboo.

SEEDS AND BEANS

Bean bear

GLUE

GLUE

1. Copy this bear on a large piece of strong paper and cut out the shape. You will need PVA glue and lots of beans, seeds, lentils and rice to decorate your bear.

2. Cover a small area of paper with lots of glue and stick on the decorations.

3. Repeat these steps until the whole bear is covered.

4. Let bean-bear dry out overnight and pin him up in your room.

DOGS

Domestic dogs are related to many other members of the dog family, such as wolves, foxes and jackals. The wolf is closest to the pet dog, as you can see if you compare a German shepherd and a grey wolf.

Wolves used to roam over many parts of the northern hemisphere, but much of their territory has been taken over by people.

There are many different kinds of foxes, including the common red fox, the fennec fox of the hot desert and the Arctic fox of the frozen north.

The dingo, the wild dog of Australia, hunts kangaroos, sheep and cattle.

The fennec is the smallest fox but it has the longest ears.

Factfile

- The whole dog family is descended from a wolf-like creature, called Tomarctus, that roamed the world's forests about 15 million years ago.
- The short-legged dachshund, or "sausage dog", used to be trained to hunt badgers.
- The coyote's scientific name, Canis latrans, means "barking dog": it is well known for its wailing howl.
- The Ancient Egyptians had dogs that looked like greyhounds.

Quiz

1 What is another name for a German shepherd dog?
2 Where would you find coyotes?
3 What is the name of the rescue dog of the Swiss Alps?
4 Which is the smallest fox with the biggest ears?
5 What is the Australian wild dog called?
6 Which breed are the world's tallest dogs?

Answers

1 Alsatian. 2 North America. 3 St Bernard.
4 Fennec fox. 5 Dingo. 6 Great Dane.

Red foxes are found all over Europe, Asia and North America.

Put a tail on the dog

1. Find or draw a large picture of a dog and put it on the wall.

2. Cut out a tail in stiff card and stick a blob of multi-purpose tac at the top.

3. Each player is blindfolded in turn and must stick the tail as close as possible to the right place on the dog.

4. Mark the spot chosen by each player – the closest is the winner.

CARDBOARD TAIL

YAP YAP

GRRRRRRR

Grey wolves live in families and hunt in packs of up to forty.

WHALES & DOLPHINS

Dolphins belong to the same family as whales. Although they spend their whole lives in the sea, whales and dolphins are not related to fish and they cannot breathe under water. They are mammals, and they come to the surface regularly to take in air through a blowhole on the top of their head.

Grey whale and calf

Some whales are huge. The killer whale is nine metres long, and the enormous blue whale is up to 33 m long – the largest animal in the world.

Killer whale

Bowhead whale

Quiz

1 What is an aquarium for dolphins called?

2 What colour is a beluga whale?

3 What is a large group of whales called?

4 Which small whale was originally called a "pig fish"?

5 Which South American river has freshwater dolphins?

6 What are baby whales called?

Answers
1 Dolphinarium.
2 White.
3 School.
4 Porpoise.
5 Amazon.
6 Calves.

ARGGHH!

Papier-mâché whale

1. Blow up a long balloon and tie a double knot in the end.
2. Tear newspaper up into strips.
3. Mix up wallpaper paste according to the instructions and paste the newspaper strips all over the balloon. Repeat the pasting until the balloon has three layers of paper. Leave it to dry for two days.
4. Paint the whale blue and stick on paper fins and a tail.

Blue whale

Minke whale

Fin whale

Factfile

- The narwhal of the Arctic is a small whale with a long single tusk sticking out in front.
- Killer whales can jump up to 5 m out of the water.
- Instead of teeth, blue whales and some others have strips of whalebone, called baleen.
- Most dolphins swim at about 30 km/h – three times faster than the best human swimmers.

BATS

There are almost a thousand different kinds of bats. They are all different from other mammals, because they can fly. They live in nearly every part of the world, except for the freezing polar regions.

Most bats are nocturnal, which means that they sleep during the day and come out at night to find food. They hang upside-down to rest and sleep, often from the roof of a cave. Most bats eat mainly insects, but some eat fruit and nectar and others hunt small animals.

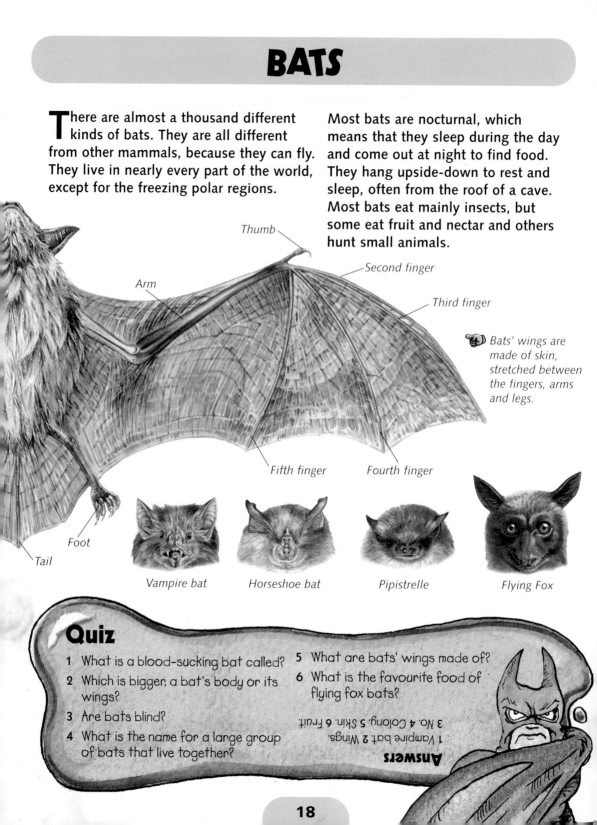

Thumb

Arm

Second finger

Third finger

Bats' wings are made of skin, stretched between the fingers, arms and legs.

Fifth finger

Fourth finger

Foot

Tail

Vampire bat

Horseshoe bat

Pipistrelle

Flying Fox

Quiz

1 What is a blood-sucking bat called?
2 Which is bigger, a bat's body or its wings?
3 Are bats blind?
4 What is the name for a large group of bats that live together?

5 What are bats' wings made of?
6 What is the favourite food of flying fox bats?

Answers
1 Vampire bat 2 Wings.
3 No. 4 Colony. 5 Skin. 6 Fruit.

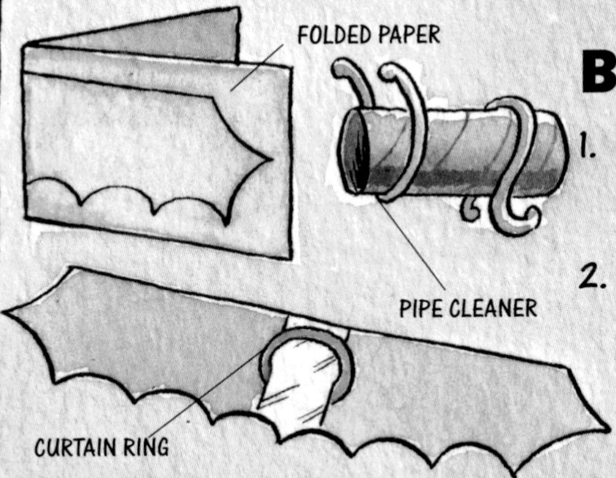

Batty bat

Labels in diagrams:
FOLDED PAPER

PIPE CLEANER

CURTAIN RING

HOOK

NYLON THREAD

1. Fold a piece of card (8 x 28 cm) in half lengthways. Copy the shape of the wing and cut it out. Don't cut the fold.

2. Use a toilet-roll tube for the body and glue pipe-cleaner legs and feelers around it.

3. Open the wings, tape a curtain ring to the wing, and glue the back of the wings to the body tube.

4. Cut a four metre length of cotton and pass the two ends through the curtain ring. Put the thread over a wall hook and pull your bat towards you along the thread. When the two ends are pulled apart, your bat will go batty.

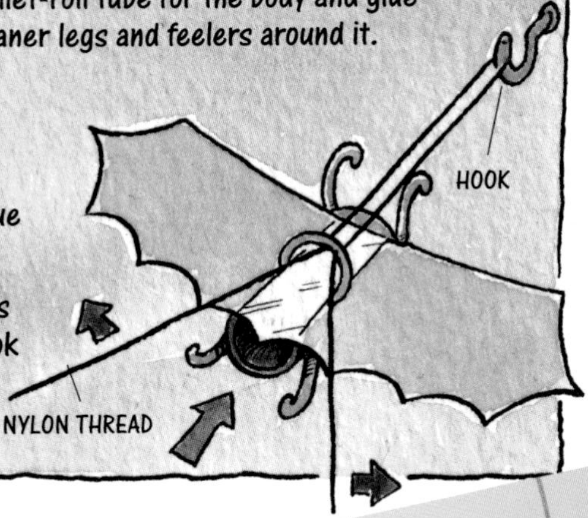

Bats detect prey using the echoes from their ultrasonic calls and clicks.

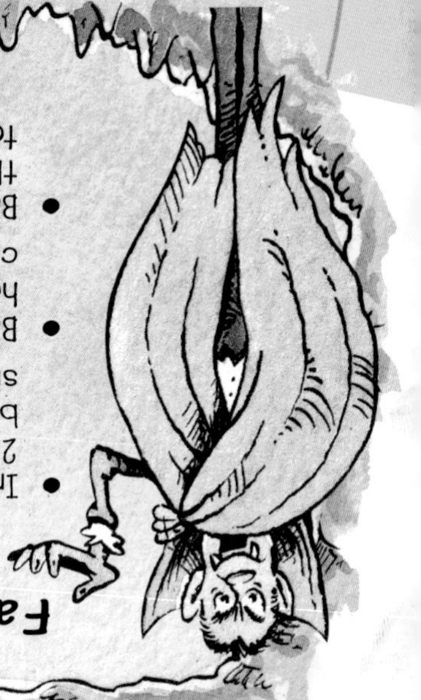

Factfile

- In a cave in Texas, USA, 20 million free-tailed bats were found in a single colony.

- Bats use their hook-shaped thumbs to climb trees and rocks.

- Bats use the echoes from their high-pitched squeaks to find their way around.

- They have large sensitive ears to pick up the echoes.

- The fisherman bat of Mexico can catch small fish with its claw-like feet.

- Little brown bats have been found living over a kilometre underground in mines.

MARSUPIALS

Marsupials are a special group of mammals. Unlike all other animals, female marsupials have a pouch. Their babies stay in the warm, snug pouch and live off their mother's milk until they are big enough to leave.

Most marsupials, such as kangaroos, koalas and wombats, live in Australia. Smaller kinds, called opossums, live in North and South America.

 Baby kangaroos are called joeys.

The wombat sleeps during the day in its burrow.

 Wallabies are like small kangaroos.

Koalas live mostly in trees, eating eucalyptus leaves.

Quiz

1 What is a male kangaroo called?
2 What's special about the water opossum's pouch?
3 What is a kangaroo's main food?
4 Which trees do koalas like best?
5 What does "playing possum" mean?
6 Which kind of rat is named after a marsupial?

Answers
1 Buck. 2 It's waterproof
3 Grass. 4 Eucalyptus.
5 Pretending to be dead.
6 Kangaroo rat

YIKES!

Factfile

- Kangaroos can jump more than 9 m in one enormous bound.
- Although they look like small bears, koalas have nothing to do with the bear family.
- Male kangaroos sometimes fight each other in a way that looks like boxing.
- Scientists discovered a previously unknown tree kangaroo in Indonesia in 1994.
- The smallest marsupial is the tiny honey possum.

Count the kangaroos

There are five roos hidden in the picture. Can you find them?

REPTILES

Scaly-skinned reptiles are a very different group of animals from mammals because they are cold-blooded. This means that reptiles always need lots of sunshine to warm them up. That is why most of them live in warm parts of the world, and some even live in hot deserts. They go into underground burrows during the hottest part of the day.

Snakes, lizards and crocodiles are all reptiles. Tortoises and turtles are reptiles whose bodies are protected by a shell.

There are more different kinds of lizards than any other sort of reptile.

65 MILLION YEARS AND STILL WE'RE EATING FLIES!

Quiz

1 What kind of reptile is a skink?

2 Where does the giant tortoise live?

3 What colour does an angry chameleon turn?

4 What kind of reptile is a loggerhead?

5 Is the lizard called a gila monster poisonous?

6 What were large prehistoric reptiles called?

Answers
1 Lizard 2 Galapagos Islands.
3 Black. 4 Turtle. 5 Yes. 6 Dinosaurs.

Chameleons are slow-moving, tree-living lizards with long, sticky tongues. Some lizards can grow a new tail if they lose their original one.

Walnut turtle

1. Split open some walnuts - each half shell makes a little turtle. If you like nuts, you could make a whole family of turtles.

2. Trace the turtle outline on card and cut it out. Paint the rim of the walnut shell with glue and fit it on the card turtle. Press the rounded part of the shell on the head of your turtle and the pointed end on the tail.

3. Wait for the glue to dry and then paint on eyes and a mouth with black felt pen.

CUT-OUT CARD

WALNUT SHELL

CAMOUFLAGE HAS MANY USES!!

Factfile

- The Komodo dragon of Indonesia, the world's largest lizard, grows up to 3 m long.

- Lizards live on land, but one kind swims in the sea – the marine iguana of the Galapagos Islands.

- Chameleons can change colour to suit their surroundings or their mood.

- The tuatara is a kind of lizard that lives in New Zealand; it belongs to an ancient family related to the dinosaurs.

SNAKES

There are more than 2,000 different kinds of snakes. They are long, legless reptiles that slither and glide forward as their bodies press against roughness in the ground. Some also climb trees, and many snakes can swim.

Snakes have forked tongues, which they flick in and out to pick up scents from the air and ground. Some snakes are poisonous, but only about 300 kinds are dangerous to people.

Poisonous snakes inject venom into their prey through a large pair of hollow teeth called fangs.

Factfile

- The world's longest snake is the reticulated python of Southeast Asia, which grows up to 10 m long.

- Emerald tree boas wrap themselves around rainforest trees and wait for prey such as birds and bats.

- A few snakes give birth to live babies, but most lay eggs with tough, leathery shells.

- One poisonous snake was found to have enough venom in it to kill a quarter of a million mice.

King snake

A rattlesnake's rattle is made up of loose scales; the rattler shakes its tail to act as a warning.

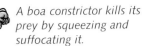
A boa constrictor kills its prey by squeezing and suffocating it.

Quiz

1 Where does the world's most poisonous snake live?

2 Is a snake's tongue poisonous?

3 Which kind of snake can rear up and spread its hood?

4 How does a boa constrictor kill?

5 Do female snakes look after their young?

6 What is the main colour of a milk snake?

Answers

1 Australia. 2 No. 3 Cobra. 4 By squeezing its victim. 5 No. 6 Red.

Stuffed snakes

HAVE YOU SEEN MY OTHER SOCK, SON?

1. Cut the legs from an old pair of tights (or use long socks) for two long snakes.

2. Stuff them with crumpled pieces of newspaper and tie the ends.

3. Cut a long forked tongue and two eyes from card or felt and stick them on.

4. Paint coloured stripes or a pattern on your stuffed snakes.

CROCODILES & ALLIGATORS

Crocodiles and alligators belong to a group of reptiles called crocodilians. They are the largest living reptiles. Powerful animals with long tails and fierce jaws, they live close to water and are found mainly in wide rivers and swamps in hot parts of the world. They often bask in the sun during the day.

When it gets dark, they slip into the water to spend the night hunting for fish and other animals.

LOOK OUT, BEHIND YOU!

Quiz

1 Do alligators lay eggs?

2 Which African river has a crocodile named after it?

3 How many different kinds of crocodilians are there – 12, 120 or 1,200?

4 On which continent does the crocodilian called a caiman live?

5 Which ancient people preserved crocodiles as mummies?

6 Which is larger, an American or a Chinese alligator?

Answers
1 Yes. 2 Nile. 3 120.
4 South America.
5 Ancient Egyptians.
6 American.

Crocodiles catch and eat fish, larger mammals and birds.

> The long body of a crocodile is covered with thick scales and bony plates along the back for protection.

Cucumber croc

1. Turn a cucumber into a fearsome crocodile. Use cocktail sticks to stick on pieces of carrot for feet and half an olive for each eye.

2. Cut a mouth and hold the jaws open with almond or apple teeth.

3. Croc's scaly back is made of cheese triangles.

CHEESE TRIANGLES

CUCUMBER BODY

OLIVES

CARROTS

ALMOND

ARGGHH!

Factfile

- Crocodiles have narrower jaws than alligators, and when their jaws are closed you can still see teeth sticking out.

- During very hot, dry weather crocodilians may bury themselves in mud and sleep until the weather changes.

- Gavials are crocodilians with long, thin snouts and about a hundred sharp teeth; they live in the big rivers of Malaysia and India.

- The estuarine or saltwater crocodiles of Asia and Australia grow up to 7 m long.

BIRDS

Birds are the only animals with feathers, and their feathered wings make them expert fliers. They live in all parts of the world, and many birds fly long distances at different parts of the year, mainly to find warm weather.

Female birds lay eggs, and most build nests to protect them. When the baby birds hatch out, their parents feed them until the youngsters can fly and safely leave the nest.

☞ *Hummingbirds flap their wings very fast to hover in the air; they use their long beak and tongue to reach for the nectar inside flowers.*

Quiz

1 Which bird lays its eggs in the nests of other birds?

2 Which bird runs fastest on the ground?

3 What is the name for a female bird?

4 Which American desert bird is known to run alongside cars?

5 What is the national bird of New Zealand?

6 Which rainforest bird is famous for its long, colourful beak?

Factfile

• The common swallow breeds in Europe, Asia and North America. Some swallows spend their winter in southern Africa and Australia.

• The Indian peacock can spread its tail feathers into a large, beautiful fan.

• Arctic terns make a round-trip of up to 36,000 km each year, flying between the frozen Arctic and Antarctic regions.

• Common swifts may stay in the air for up to four years, sleeping on the wing.

• The smallest bird is the bee hummingbird of Cuba, which is less than 6 cm long.

Answers 1 Cuckoo. 2 Ostrich. 3 Hen. 4 Roadrunner. 5 Kiwi. 6 Toucan.

28

Birds beat their wings to improve the airflow past their wings. This helps them fly.

The wandering albatross has the biggest wingspan of any bird – up to 3.6 m.

The ostrich is the world's largest bird.

ON YOUR MARKS!

Flying high

1. Make a paper-bag kite. Punch holes 4 cm from the edge of each of the four corners of a large paper bag. Stick paper ring reinforcements on each hole.

2. Cut two pieces of string and tie each end into a hole to make two loops. Tie a long piece of string through the two loops to form a handle.

3. Decorate your kite. Glue on a paper tissue tail.

4. Hold onto the string and run so the wind catches in the bag.

STRING

TISSUE PAPER

PAPER BAG

BIRDS OF PREY

We call birds that hunt animals for food birds of prey. Eagles, hawks and falcons are all daytime hunters. They are fast fliers and have excellent eyesight, so that they can swoop down on their prey from a great height. They grab the victim with their powerful talons and tear it apart with their hooked beaks.

Owls hunt mostly at night, catching small mammals such as mice and voles. Vultures don't normally hunt at all, but live off scraps of dead creatures killed by other animals.

An owl's wing feathers have a soft fringe, which helps the owl fly almost silently and surprise its unsuspecting prey.

Roly-poly owl

1. Make two small holes at the top of an empty yoghurt pot. Push a piece of plastic drinking straw through one side of the pot, through the centre of a cotton reel and out through the other hole of the pot. Fix the ends of the straw with masking tape to stop them slipping out.

2. Cut out six circles (three for each eye) and stick them on the pot. Make wings from pleated sheets of paper, and glue on paper claws and a beak.

COTTON REEL

YOGHURT POT

FOLDED PAPER

Factfile

- The lammergeier, or bearded vulture, drops bones onto rocks to split them open and get at the marrow inside.

- The peregrine falcon is the world's fastest bird; it dives at up to 350 km/h.

- The Egyptian vulture drops stones onto ostrich eggs to crack them open.

- The North American elf owl is just 13 cm long.

- Vultures have been recorded flying at a height of over 11,000 m, as high as a jet plane.

Sharp eyes with excellent long-distance vision

Nostril

Hooked beak, good for tearing meat

Vulture

☞ *Lammergeier dropping bones onto the rocks below*

Quiz

1 Which bird of prey has the same name as a flying toy?

2 What is the main food of the osprey?

3 Which eagle is the emblem of the USA?

4 Which is the biggest bird of prey?

5 What was the royal bird of the Middle Ages?

6 Which owl lives near the North Pole?

1 Kite. 2 Fish. 3 Bald eagle.
4 Condor. 5 Golden eagle.
6 Snowy owl.

Answers

ARE YOU SURE THIS WIG WILL STAY ON AT 100 METRES?

PENGUINS

Penguins are birds, but they cannot fly. Their feathers are short and thick, and these help keep penguins warm in cold seas and on frozen shores. Penguins have a small pair of wings, which act as flippers for swimming rather than flying.

They spend much of their time at sea feeding on fish, squid and small shrimp-like krill. Penguins live near the coasts of the cold southern oceans, and many never leave the frozen region of Antarctica.

There are just 3,000 yellow eyed penguins left in the world.

Emperor penguins are the biggest, at up to 120 cm tall.

Quiz

1 What is a baby penguin called?

2 Rockhopper penguins hop from rock to rock – true or false?

3 What is the name of the only African penguin?

4 Are there any penguins at the North Pole?

5 What do penguins use as rudders when they swim?

6 What do we call a colony of penguins?

Answers
1 Chick. 2 True. 3 Jackass penguin. 4 No. 5 Their feet. 6 A rookery.

Penguin sock puppet

1. Put your hand into a black sock, so you can work the head with your fingers.

2. Tie or glue a piece of white cloth around the penguin's neck and glue on button eyes.

3. Take the sock off and cut holes on either side. Make a cone beak out of card and attach it with some thread. Push your thumb and little finger through the holes to make the flippers.

Rockhopper penguins have long feathers above their eyes.

Magellanic penguins are found around the freezing coasts of Antarctica.

4,205... 4,206... 4,207... ER.. OH NO! 1,2,3,4.

Factfile

- Emperor penguins put their eggs and chicks on their feet, to keep them warm.

- There are 18 species, or different kinds, of penguin; six species breed in Antarctica, the ice-covered continent around the South Pole.

- The little blue penguin of Australia and New Zealand is the smallest of all, standing 40 cm high.

- Gentoos can swim at up to 27 km/h.

- Penguins sometimes slide along on their body instead of walking; we call this tobogganing.

- Penguins can dive down over 450 m under-water and stay under for 18 minutes.

AMPHIBIANS

Amphibians are animals that spend part of their lives on land and part in water. They include frogs, toads, newts and salamanders. Amphibians go to water when it is time to lay their eggs. Females usually lay their eggs in or near a pond or stream.

Most frogs lay between 1,000 and 20,000 eggs in a mass of jelly. We call these large clusters of eggs spawn. Like many amphibians, frogs go through different stages before they become adults.

① Frog spawn floats on top of fresh water.

② Tadpoles hatch from the eggs.

④ The froglet loses its tail and grows into an adult frog.

③ Tadpoles grow legs and change into froglets.

Factfile

- Toads usually have a rougher, bumpier skin than frogs, and they can live in drier places.

- Tree frogs have round suckers on their toes, which help them to grip.

- Big North American bullfrogs can catch mice or even small snakes.

- South American sharp-nosed frogs can jump over 3 m.

I HOPE I DON'T MEET A GIANT SALAMANDER!

Quiz

1 What does a tadpole turn into?

2 Which are better jumpers, frogs or toads?

3 How big is a giant salamander – 3, 30 or 300 cm long?

4 Can you get warts from handling a toad?

5 Where do mouth-brooding frogs keep their eggs?

6 What kind of amphibian is a hellbender?

Toads hibernate on land during the winter.

Newts swim by lashing their tails.

CUT-OUT 'FLIES'

Feed a frog

1. Make your own pet frog and feed him a swarm of homemade flies.

2. Copy this frog's face onto a large piece of card. Colour it in and cut it out. Carefully cut out the frog's big mouth. For a backing use a piece of green crêpe paper and glue the face to it, making sure the mouth stays open. Tie a line between two chairs and peg your frog up by the crêpe paper. Your frog is now ready to be fed.

3. To make some tasty flies, fold some small pieces of card in half. Draw a wing shape on each piece and cut it out.

4. Stand a metre or two away from your frog and try to throw the flies into its mouth. You could play this game with a friend and count how many flies your frog can catch.

FOLDED PAPER

FISH

There are more than 20,000 different kinds of fish in the world's oceans, lakes and rivers, from the tiniest freshwater minnow to the biggest ocean-going shark. Fish have gills instead of lungs, which allow them to breathe underwater.

Eels have snakelike bodies and very small fins.

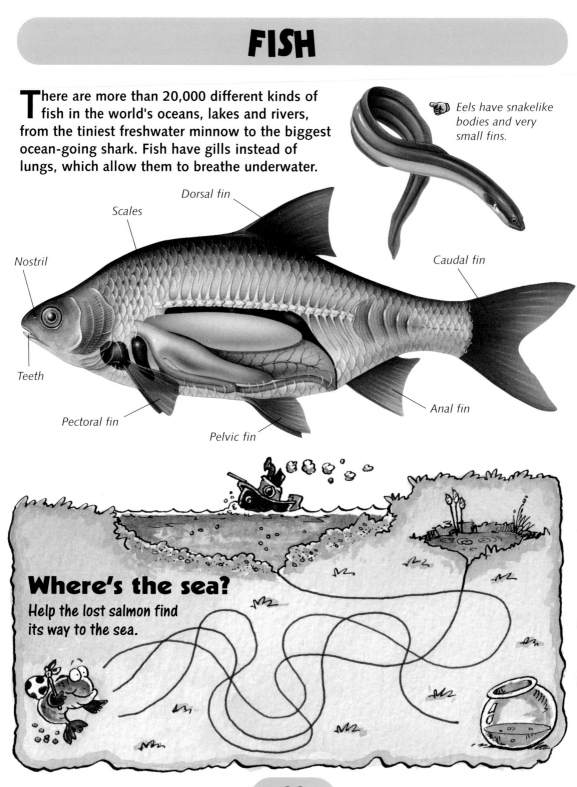

Dorsal fin

Scales

Nostril

Caudal fin

Teeth

Anal fin

Pectoral fin

Pelvic fin

Where's the sea?

Help the lost salmon find its way to the sea.

QUICK
LEGGIT!

Quiz

1 Which are real fish – catfish, dogfish, parrotfish?

2 Which South American meat-eating fish has the strongest, sharpest teeth?

3 Which is not a trout – brown, rainbow, sockeye?

4 To which fish family does the goldfish belong?

5 A kipper is a smoked what?

6 Which special food comes from the sturgeon?

Answers

1 All of them. 2 Piranha.
3 Sockeye (it's a salmon).
4 Carp. 5 Herring.
6 Caviar.

Flying fish have pectoral fins shaped like wings.

Rays have flat bodies, which help them glide along the bottom of the sea.

Factfile

- The fastest fish is the sailfish, which can swim at over 100 km/h.

- The porcupine fish swells up into a spiny ball when it senses danger nearby.

- Rays feed mainly on shellfish, which they crack open with their strong teeth; some rays can sting with their tails.

- Electric eels kill fish and other sea animals with electric shocks from their tail.

- Flying fish have large pectoral fins, which they use to jump out of the water and fly for a distance of up to 150 m.

CLOSER... CLOSER...
THAT'S IT!

SHARKS

People are fascinated by sharks. They are very frightened of them, too, though many sharks are quite harmless. Nevertheless, sharks are the fierce hunters of the world's oceans. They have big, strong jaws and teeth, and when they attack other fish or dolphins, they show amazing speed and power.

Unlike other fish, a shark's skeleton is made of rubbery cartilage instead of bone. Sharks also do not have a swim bladder, which means they have to keep swimming all the time, or they sink to the bottom.

The great white shark, famous as "Jaws", normally grows up to 6 m long.

Starry
Smoothhound

Chase the shark

A racing game for two players.

1. Cut out two tissue-paper sharks. Each one should be about 30 cm long. Stick on eyes.

2. Lie the sharks flat on their backs. Place two plates about three metres away on the other side of the room. Hit the ground just behind the shark with a rolled-up newspaper to make it move. The shark that lands on the plate first is the winner.

ROLLED-UP
NEWSPAPER

TISSUE PAPER

Sandbar shark

The blue shark is a slender fish, with very long pectoral fins and a pointed snout.

Quiz

1 Which shark has a tail as long as its body?

2 Which one does not exist – basking shark, lion shark, or tiger shark?

3 How many gill slits do most sharks have?

4 A dogfish is a small shark – true or false?

5 Are hammerhead sharks dangerous to people?

6 How many different kinds of sharks are there – 25, 125 or 250?

Factfile

● Some female sharks lay eggs in a tough case which we call a mermaid's purse.

● The whale shark is the world's biggest fish, growing over 12 m long, but it is not at all dangerous.

● The world's smallest shark is the dwarf shark, which is just 15 cm long.

● Sharks have an excellent sense of smell and good hearing, which helps them in their hunting.

● The wobbegong, or carpet shark, lies flat and camouflaged on the bottom of the sea.

Answers

1 Thresher shark. 2 Lion shark. 3 Five. 4 True. 5 Yes. 6 250.

39

INSECTS

There are more than a million different kinds of insects in the world. This group of tiny animals accounts for over three-quarters of all animal species on Earth, and more insects are being discovered and named all the time. Insects have no backbone, but are protected by a hard outer skeleton or shell. All insects have six legs, and most have wings and can fly.

Because they are so small, insects can fit into tiny spaces and need little food to live on.

Antennae, or feelers, detect movements of the air, vibrations and smells.

Compound eyes are made up of hundreds of tiny lenses.

Legs and wings are attached to the thorax.

The large abdomen contains many of the insect's organs, such as the heart.

Termites build huge mounds as nests for their colony. Each colony is ruled by a king and a queen.

Ants have very strong jaws and can give a painful bite. Some kinds squirt formic acid into the wound made by their bite, adding to the effect!

Ants live in colonies, which may contain up to 100,000 insects.

Factfile

- Wasps and other insects usually sting to defend themselves and their nests.

- Other insects, such as mosquitoes, are bloodsuckers; they stick a needle-like tube into the skin and suck up a tiny amount of blood.

- A single bee would have to visit more than 4,000 flowers to make one tablespoon of honey.

- When they grow into winged adults, mayflies may live for no more than an hour.

- The fastest flying insects have been timed at 39 km/h.

Honey bees collect nectar and pollen from flowers. They take this food to their nest, where it is stored as honey.

Tissue bugs

1. Screw up tissue paper into a tight ball. Wrap the ball into another piece of tissue paper and hold it together with sticky tape. Paint on eyes and tape on pipe cleaner legs.

2. Paint the ladybird's body red and add black spots. Paint three pipe cleaners black and tape them on to make three legs on each side.

3. You could make other bugs in the same way.

COME ON... BEDTIME WAS OVER 20 MINUTES AGO.

Quiz

1 What kind of insect is a ladybird?
2 Which mosquitoes "bite", male or female?
3 Which insect is called a white ant?
4 How many pairs of wings do most insects have?
5 What are animals without a backbone called?
6 Which insects jump furthest?

Answers

1 Beetle. 2 Female. 3 Termite. 4 Two.
5 Invertebrates. 6 Fleas.

BUTTERFLIES

Like many insects, butterflies change their bodies as they develop. These changes are called metamorphosis.

Butterfly eggs develop into caterpillars. Each caterpillar turns into a chrysalis, and the final stage is a beautiful butterfly. Butterflies have thin, delicate wings, and most are brightly coloured. They usually fly about and feed during the day.

Most moths have a duller colour and fly at night.

Caterpillars feed on the leaves of a plant. Then they turn into a chrysalis, or pupa, which often hangs from a plant.

Female butterflies lay their eggs in a batch on a plant. Each egg hatches into a butterfly.

Egg

Caterpillar

Chrysalis

Fully formed butterfly

Emerging butterfly

When the butterfly first emerges from the chrysalis, its wings are soft and crumpled.

Butterfly prints

- Drop blots of different coloured paint in the middle of a sheet of paper. Fold the paper in half and press it down.

PAINT BLOBS

FOLDED PAPER

- Open up the folded paper and admire your butterfly.

- Cut the butterfly out and hang it on your wall. Now it won't fly away!

Factfile

- The caterpillar stage of a butterfly is its larva; we often call insect larvae grubs or maggots.

- The world's largest butterfly is the Queen Alexandra's birdwing, which has a wingspan of more than 28 cm.

- The smallest butterflies have a wingspan of just 6 mm.

- When a butterfly rests, it holds its wings upright; a moth folds its wings flat over its body.

- Monarch butterflies have been found to travel more than 3,000 km; some butterflies fly all the way across the Atlantic Ocean.

Quiz

1 Are male and female butterflies always the same colour?

2 What do clothes moth larvae love to chew?

3 What is a butterfly's feeding tube called?

4 Is the red admiral a butterfly or a moth?

5 Which is not a moth – old lady, moon, swallowtail?

6 What colour is a cabbage butterfly?

Answers
1 No. 2 Wool. 3 Proboscis. 4 Butterfly. 5 Swallowtail (it's a butterfly). 6 White.

ONLY TWO MORE STAGES AND YOU'LL BE ABLE TO FLY!!

Antennae

Compound eyes

Upper wing

Lower wing

SPIDERS

Spiders are similar to insects, but they belong to a different group of animals called arachnids. All arachnids have eight legs. Many spiders spin silky webs, which they use to catch flies and other small insects. Spiders have fangs for seizing their prey, and most paralyze their victims with poison before they kill and eat them. Fortunately, only a few spiders are poisonous to humans.

(1) *The spider's silk comes from inside its body. The spider starts a web by building a bridge.*

(2) *Then it makes a triangle shape.*

(3) *It adds more threads to make a complete framework.*

(4) *Finally, the spider fills the frame with circular threads.*

(5) *A spider's web is strong enough to catch large insects, but it is easily damaged by larger animals and people.*

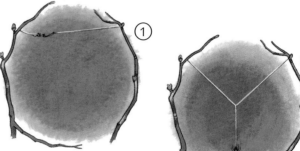

Factfile

- Scorpions, ticks and mites are also arachnids.

- Most spiders and other arachnids have eight eyes, but they still don't see very well.

- In a grassy meadow, there may be as many as 500 spiders in a square metre.

- Female spiders lay up to 2,000 eggs, which they wrap in a bundle of silk threads.

- The world's largest spider is the goliath bird-eating spider of South America, which has a leg span of 28 cm.

Quiz

1 How many more legs has a spider got than an ant?

2 What are baby spiders called?

3 Which golden orb-web spider weighs more, male or female?

4 Where is a scorpion's sting?

5 How many different kinds of spiders are there – 400, 4,000, or 40,000?

6 What colour is the ----- widow spider?

Tarantulas have long 👉 hairy legs and a deadly bite.

👉 Spiders use their beautifully made webs to catch insects.

The trapdoor spider digs a burrow and covers it with a door. Then it waits in the burrow. When an insect passes by, the spider feels the ground move and jumps out. It catches the insect and drags it into the burrow.

Wool web

1. Weave white wool around a starshaped construction of twigs.

2. Cut out a black paper spider and hide it in the web.

3. Hang up the spider's web and see what you catch!

TWIGS

WOOL

MOLLUSCS & CRUSTACEANS

Many molluscs live in the sea, but some live on land. Many marine molluscs, such as the octopus, have soft bodies. Others, such as land and sea snails, and shellfish such as cockles, mussels and oysters, are protected by hard shells.

Crustaceans got their name from their crusty covering. Most of them, such as crabs, lobsters and shrimps, live in the sea. A few crustaceans, such as woodlice, live on land.

Octopus

Squid

Hermit crab

Modelling dough creatures

1. Use different coloured modelling dough or make your own with two cups flour, one cup salt, one tablespoon cooking oil, one cup water (with added food colouring).

2. Mix the flour and salt, then add the oil and water. Knead well.

3. Roll out a sausage shape for a snail, use two matchstick ends for its tentacles. Mould a crab and an octopus.

46

Factfile

- Squids and octopuses shoot out inky fluid to cloud the water when they want to get away from enemies.

- The largest crustacean is the giant spider crab, which has a leg-span of almost 4 m.

- The smallest crustaceans are water fleas, which measure less than 0.25 mm.

- Octopuses can change colour according to their surroundings, so they can easily hide.

- The largest bivalve shellfish is the giant clam, which grows up to 115 cm long.

Quiz

1. What does a snail have that a slug doesn't?

2. Do crabs walk frontwards, backwards or sideways?

3. How many legs does a shrimp have?

4. Is a cuttlefish a fish, a mollusc or a crustacean?

5. Which valuable gems grow in oysters?

6. Are there more kinds of land snails or sea snails?

Answers

1 A shell. 2 Sideways.
3 Ten. 4 Mollusc. 5 Pearls.
6 Sea snails.

Lobster

Snail

HOW ABOUT A BIT OF ARMED COMBAT?

47

Index